LANCASHIRE COUNTY LIBRARY

D0784458

Lancashire Library Services	
30118134742570	
PETERS	J796GRY
£6.99	05-Jun-2017
CPP	

Bear Grylls

SURVIVAL SKILLS HANDBOOK

DANGERS AND EMERGENCIES

Bear Grylls

This survival handbook has been specially put together to help young adventurers just like you to stay safe in the wild. There is so much out there to explore and experience, yet it is vital that you remain unharmed as you pursue new adventures. Our planet and its creatures can be dangerous at times, so learn the skills you need, and remain safe in the face of adversity.

Bear.

CONTENTS

STAY SAFE IN THE WILD

When you set out on an adventure it is very important to be fully prepared in case you come into contact with danger. There are many ways to get help and avoid harm, so do your homework and stay safe.

Signalling for help

In an emergency your first contact with the outside world is likely to be a search aircraft. Make this contact count by learning standard ground-to-air signals. You can use objects, as well as your own body, to seek help.

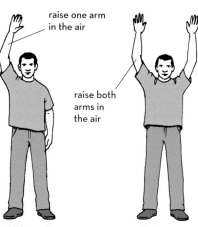

raise one arm in the air

raise both arms in the air

All is well

Pick us up

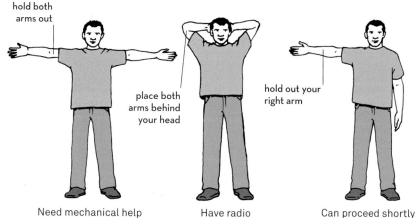

hold both arms out

place both arms behind your head

hold out your right arm

Need mechanical help

Have radio

Can proceed shortly

lay down with both your arms above your head

Need medical help

raise both arms in the air and wave them

Do not attempt to land here

bend your knees and hold both arms out in front of you, pointing in the direction of landing

Land here

BEAR SAYS

If you are in distress, these signals could save your life. Choose a large, open area where you are most likely to be seen.

wave a piece of material from side to side

hold one arm out and wave it up and down

wave a piece of material up and down

Use drop message

Negative (no)

Affirmative (yes)

Fire cones
Keep these primed with plenty of dry fuel, and ready to go at all times.

Smoke cones
In the daytime, smoke marks your position more clearly than fire. Use fuel sources such as green branches and rubber.

BEAR SAYS
Wherever you are in the world, three objects together signal distress. Don't forget this international call for help!

Life rafts
In thick jungle, the only clear area may be a river. Tether together three rafts loaded with fuel for a jungle distress signal.

Smoke flare

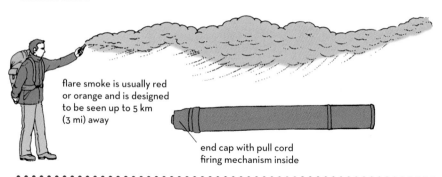

flare smoke is usually red
or orange and is designed
to be seen up to 5 km
(3 mi) away

end cap with pull cord
firing mechanism inside

Other types of signals

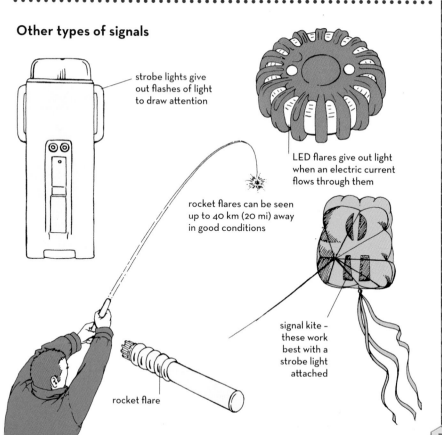

strobe lights give
out flashes of light
to draw attention

LED flares give out light
when an electric current
flows through them

rocket flares can be seen
up to 40 km (20 mi) away
in good conditions

signal kite –
these work
best with a
strobe light
attached

rocket flare

Signal mirror

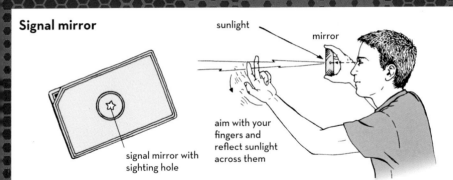

sunlight

mirror

aim with your fingers and reflect sunlight across them

signal mirror with sighting hole

A mirror is the most valuable means of signalling in daylight, as reflections can easily attract attention. Make sure to pack one if you are going off the beaten track.

Personal locator beacons

High-tech personal locator beacons (PLBs) are small, lightweight devices that can be used in an emergency anywhere in the world. First of all, the PLB is activated (1), then a signal is sent to a satellite network in space (2). A ground station then receives the signal relayed by a satellite (3). The search and rescue coordination centre is alerted (4) and then help is sent (5).

PLB

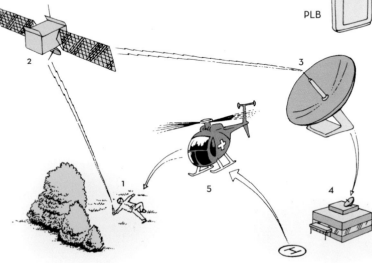

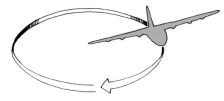
Aircraft signals

A rocking wing
If a plane rocks its wings the pilot has understood your signal.

Flying clockwise
This manoeuvre indicates that your signal is not understood.

Prepare a helicopter landing zone

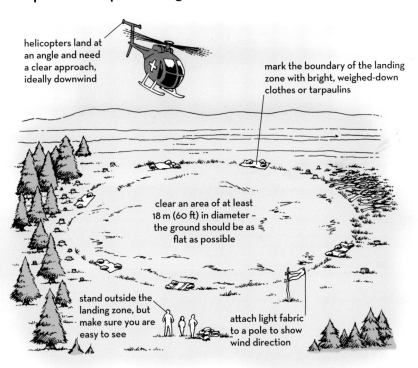

helicopters land at an angle and need a clear approach, ideally downwind

mark the boundary of the landing zone with bright, weighed-down clothes or tarpaulins

clear an area of at least 18 m (60 ft) in diameter – the ground should be as flat as possible

stand outside the landing zone, but make sure you are easy to see

attach light fabric to a pole to show wind direction

DANGEROUS ANIMALS

Most creatures will avoid human contact, but it pays to know what species are dangerous and what your defences are.

Insects

Insects are small, often winged animals with six legs. Most are harmless, but some can be deadly.

Bee

A bee sting is painful but only life-threatening to those who are allergic. If you are attacked by a swarm of bees, run away from the point of first contact, protect your face, and seek shelter.

Ant

Ant stings range from harmless to agonizing. Be sure to avoid the bullet ant of Central and South America. Its sting is considered the most painful of any bee, wasp, or ant.

Wasps and hornets

Relatives of bees and ants, these insects can sting over and over. They can be aggressive when seeking food, and are drawn to sweet odours. Stay away from nests as allergic reactions can be fatal.

Mosquito

The mosquito is one of the deadliest creatures on Earth. Mosquito-borne diseases are a big problem in the tropics, but can occur in temperate regions too.

Flea

A flea bite is normally just an irritation, but they can lead to many diseases, including Lyme disease and even bubonic plague. It is sensible to consider them as a threat.

Tsetse flies

These large, blood-sucking insects are found in Africa between the Sahara and the Kalahari deserts. They carry the parasite that causes sleeping sickness, which can be fatal.

adult   larva

Botfly

An egg of the human botfly (native to Mexico, Central, and South America) hatches when it detects human warmth. The larva then burrows into the skin where it grows for about eight weeks. They may cause painful swellings but are otherwise harmless.

How to remove a botfly larva

1 The larva needs to breathe, so cut off its air supply by covering it with duct tape.

2 Apply pressure around the wound and grasp the larva tail with tweezers when it comes out.

3 Pull until the larva is completely out. Clean and bandage the wound.

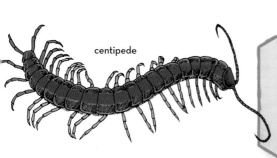

centipede

BEAR SAYS

Centipedes, especially the larger species, can inflict painful, venomous bites. If bitten, clean the wound and seek help.

Arachnids

Arachnids have eight legs and a body made up of two parts. These are some of the most dangerous kinds.

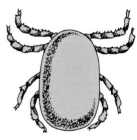

BEAR SAYS

To remove a tick, use thin tweezers, and grasp the tick as close to the skin as possible. Pull upwards with a steady, even pressure.

Hard tick

These tiny bloodsucking arachnids are responsible for the spread of many illnesses. The hard tick family comprises the majority of tick species. They have a hard shield-like plate just behind their mouthparts.

Soft tick

The less common soft ticks have a rounded, leathery appearance with mouthparts that can't be seen from above. They feed mostly on birds and small mammals, but will also choose human hosts.

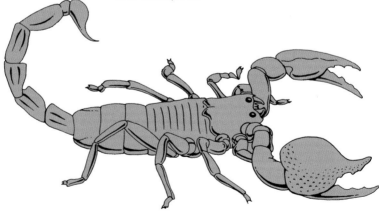

Scorpion

About 25 species of scorpions can kill. They live in northern Africa, the Middle East, India, Mexico, and parts of South America. Most of the other 1,000 or so species can deliver a very painful sting.

Funnel-web spider

There are about 40 species of funnel-web spiders in Australia. The highly venomous Sydney funnel-web spider is possibly the world's most dangerous spider. It is likely to strike repeatedly if disturbed.

Widow spider

Many spiders in this animal group are highly venomous. Well-known species include the black widow (North America), the redback spider (Australia) and button spiders (southern Africa). Bites can be deadly.

Brazilian wandering spider

This group of aggressive spiders is found in Central and South America, and in banana shipments worldwide. Their venom is the most toxic of any spider.

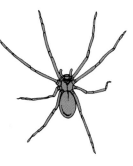

Recluse spider

Bites from these spiders can cause cell tissue death requiring skin grafts and other surgery in extreme cases. Mild skin damage and itchiness is more common, however.

Tarantula

These frightening-looking spiders are actually quite timid. Most bites are similar to a wasp sting, although one species causes hallucinations. Some kinds shed irritating hairs as a form of defence.

Reptiles

Cold-blooded creatures, such as reptiles are covered with scales or bony plates. Snakes and lizards belong to this group – and many can deliver a potentially fatal bite.

American snakes

Copperhead
These well-camouflaged North American snakes will often freeze when feeling threatened. This means that bites often happen when they are stepped on by accident. Luckily, their bites are rarely fatal.

Rattlesnake
These snakes cause the majority of snake injuries and deaths in North America (even so, deaths are very rare). Despite their deadly reputation, rattlesnakes are timid, normally giving a warning rattle when alarmed.

Bushmaster
This genus of large venomous vipers is found in remote forested areas of Central and South America. The bushmaster is capable of repeated strikes and the injection of large amounts of venom.

Cottonmouth
This viper is native to the south-eastern United States. A cottonmouth will vibrate its tail and throw its mouth open as a threat display. Bites are painful and can be fatal.

Coral snake
There are over 65 recognized species of coral snakes in the Americas. They have very potent venom, but because of their mild nature and small fangs, deaths and injuries are rare. Many harmless snakes mimic the coral snakes' colouration for protection.

African and Asian snakes

Boomslang

The venom of this sub-Saharan snake works as a hemotoxin – even small amounts will cause severe internal and external bleeding. They will strike fast if disturbed.

Cobra

Most cobra species rear up and spread their necks in a threat display. Some can "spit" venom up to 2.5 m (8 ft). They aim for their attacker's eyes. A direct hit causes severe burning pain.

Krait

This group of snakes is found in the jungles of India and Southeast Asia. They are armed with a neurotoxin that causes muscle paralysis (loss of movement).

Saw-scaled viper

These small snakes live in dry savannah habitats. They make a rasping sound when alarmed by rubbing the sides of their bodies together. They are very dangerous.

Puff adder

This snake species is responsible for more snake bite deaths in Africa than any other. When approached, it draws its head close to its coils, makes a loud hissing sound and is quick to strike.

Mamba

Most mamba species are tree-dwelling. The exception is the land-based black mamba – the world's fastest, and Africa's deadliest, snake. Untreated, its bite is fatal.

Australian snakes

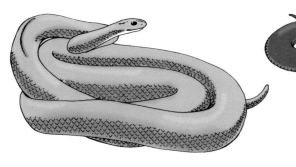

Eastern brown snake

This snake species is responsible for most deaths caused by snakebite in Australia. Its venom is the most toxic of any land snake in the world, except for the inland taipan.

Red-bellied black

The red-bellied black is commonly found in woodlands, forests, swamplands, and urban areas of eastern Australia. They usually avoid attack. Bites are dangerous but rarely fatal.

Taipan

All species in this group are dangerous. The inland taipan is viewed as the most venomous land snake in the world. However, the human population of its habitat is low, and all bite victims have been successfully treated with antivenom.

Tiger snake

The common tiger snake is found in Southern and Eastern Australia. Their highly toxic venom is produced in large amounts. The venom mainly affects the central nervous system, but also causes muscle damage, and affects blood clotting.

Death adder

Death adders are found in most parts of Australia, New Guinea, and nearby islands. They have relatively large fangs and toxic venom. Before the introduction of antivenom, about 60 per cent of bites to humans were fatal.

Sea snakes

Hydrophiinae

Found in warm coastal waters from the Indian Ocean to the Pacific, some species have venom more toxic than any land snake. Sea snakes are curious and will readily approach divers and swimmers, but they are generally placid and unlikely to attack.

European snakes

Adder

The common adder is the only poisonous snake of Northern Europe. It is widespread in highly populated areas, and bites are fairly common – but very rarely fatal. The common adder has several larger and more dangerous relatives in southern Europe.

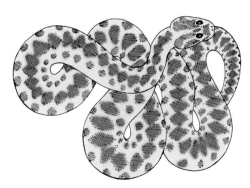

BEAR SAYS

Snake venom can be deadly. It can contain neurotoxins that affect the body's nervous system, or hemotoxins that destroy red blood cells. Stay away!

Avoiding snakebites

Snakes are timid creatures. Unless they are stepped on, cornered, or handled, they present very little danger to humans. When you are in their habitat, follow these tips to avoid a bite.

carry a stick and use it to push aside logs and shrubbery

stout boots and gaiters will protect vulnerable body parts low to the ground

keep to cleared tracks as much as possible

Treating snakebites

1 Snakebites usually occur on a limb. Start applying a pressure bandage just above the toes or fingers.

2 Continue as far up the limb as possible. This slows the movement of the venom and the onset of symptoms.

3 Apply a splint to the limb and keep it below the level of the heart. Keep the victim calm and make sure their breathing is regular.

Lizards

Gila monster

This venomous species is native to the south-western US and the north-western Mexican state of Sonora. Although a Gila bite is extremely painful, none has resulted in a confirmed human death.

BEAR SAYS

It is rare for a snake to actually chase a person, so if you come across one in the wild, stay calm and back away slowly.

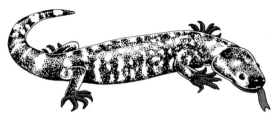

Beaded lizard

A close relative of the Gila monster, the beaded lizard is found mostly in Mexico and southern Guatemala. Its bite causes terrible pain, swelling, and a rapid drop in blood pressure.

Crocodile

Two crocodile species – the Nile crocodile and the saltwater crocodile – are maneaters. Stay well away from water where they are known to be present.

Alligator

The American alligator is native to the south-eastern US. Alligators occasionally attack unprovoked, and their bites can cause dangerous infections.

Aquatic animals

Our oceans, rivers, and lakes can be deadly places. Knowing and recognizing these creatures is highly important if you are spending time near water.

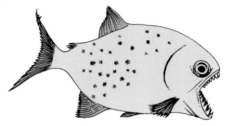

Piranha

The mouths of these South American freshwater fish are packed with sharp triangular teeth that can puncture and rip. While they will not strip humans to the bone, piranhas will take bites of flesh and remove toes.

Candiru

The Amazon's most feared fish usually survives by invading the gills of larger fish, where it feeds on blood. However, it has also been known to lodge itself in the human urethra (the tube that connects the bladder to the outside of the body).

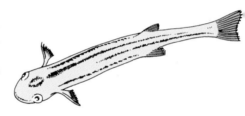

Bull shark

This shark species lives in both the open ocean and hundreds of miles up rivers. Because of their wide habitat range and aggression, many experts consider them the most dangerous shark species.

Electric eel

When angry, these large South American fish can deliver a burst of 600 volts – more than enough to kill. However, such deaths are very rare.

334555555

Flower urchin

Many sea urchins are armed with sharp spines and should be avoided. The spines of a flower urchin inject an extremely toxic venom. Injuries are very painful, and deaths have been reported.

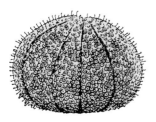

Box jellyfish

These deadly jellyfish live in coastal waters off northern Australia and throughout the Indo-Pacific. A box jellyfish sting is so excruciating and overwhelming that a victim can go into shock and drown if swimming alone. Heart failure often follows.

Portuguese man-of-war

The sting of the Portuguese man-of-war causes severe pain and in some cases, fever and shock as well as heart and breathing problems. To treat, remove any stingers that are still attached, wash with seawater, then submerge the affected area in hot water.

Cone shell

These pretty marine snails use unique venoms to hunt their prey. A sting from a large cone shell brings severe pain and is potentially fatal. Treat as though it is a snakebite – there is no antivenom cure.

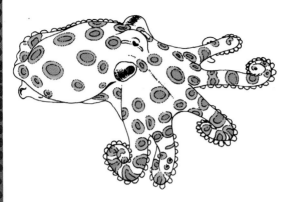

Blue-ringed octopus

These octopus live in tide pools in the Pacific Ocean from Japan to Australia. Although small and docile, they carry enough venom to kill 26 adults within minutes. Stings can bring total paralysis without loss of consciousness. Victims require artificial respiration for survival.

Needle fish

These shallow marine-dwelling fish make short jumps out of the water at speeds up to 65 km/h (40 mph). Their sharp beaks can inflict deep wounds and often break off inside the victim.

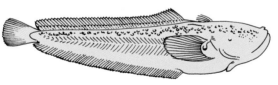

Toadfish

Venomous toadfish dwell in tropical waters off the coasts of Central and South America. They have very sharp, very poisonous spines hidden in their dorsal fins. They bury themselves in the sand and are easily stepped on.

Stonefish

The world's most venomous fish, live in the coastal waters of the tropical Indo-Pacific. Symptoms of its venom are muscle weakness, temporary paralysis, and shock, which may cause death if not treated.

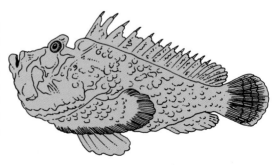

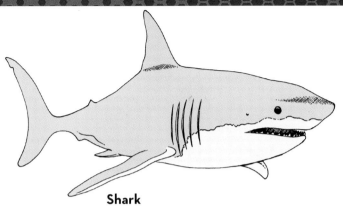

Shark

Although greatly feared, shark attacks on humans are extremely rare. No species is thought to target people as prey. Only a few kinds (the great white, tiger, and bull shark) have been involved in a significant number of fatal, unprovoked attacks.

Lionfish

This genus of aggressive fish is native to the tropical Indo-Pacific and has been introduced into the Atlantic coastal waters of the United States. Its venom can result in vomiting, fever, and sweating, and has been lethal in a few cases.

Stingray

These fish are mostly gentle, yet have a venomous barbed sting on the tail. People are usually stung accidentally when stepping on a stingray. Stings can result in pain, swelling, nausea, and muscle cramps.

Mammals

Mammals are warm-blooded animals that have fur or hair on their bodies, and they feed their babies with milk. Some large mammals, such as these, can be particularly threatening if disturbed.

American black bear
These medium-sized bears rarely attack humans but you should still avoid contact if possible. The most dangerous black bears are those that are hungry or have become used to human contact.

Brown bear
These large bears are normally unpredictable, and will attack if they are surprised or feel threatened. Mothers with cubs are particularly dangerous. If attacked, protect the back of the neck and play dead.

Polar bear
Contact with the world's largest land carnivore, or meat eater, should be avoided. A well-fed polar bear may show signs of curiosity near humans, while a hungry bear may stalk, kill, and eat you. Escape is unlikely without a weapon, but you could curl up and play dead.

Vampire bat

The common vampire bat is native to the American tropics and subtropics. They will feed on human blood when horse and cattle are in short supply. Their bites can cause rabies, a deadly viral infection.

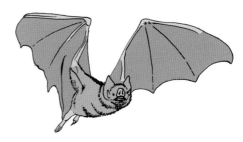

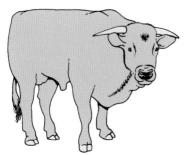

Bull

There is nothing like a large bull to turn a pleasant walk into a frightening ordeal. Never turn your back on a bull that has its head lowered or is pawing the ground. Back away slowly.

Rhinoceros

The five living species of rhinoceros are known for charging without being provoked. With very poor eyesight, they often panic at unusual smells and sounds.

BEAR SAYS

Never anger a hippopotamus! They are responsible for more human deaths in Africa than any other large animal.

Tiger
The tiger is the largest of the cat species. Human prey appears to be a last resort for tigers, but individual man-eaters have been responsible for hundreds of deaths.

Lion
As with tigers, humans are not a favoured prey of lions. However, where human settlements encroach on lion territory and regular prey animals are in short supply, lions will hunt and kill humans.

Leopard
Attacks by leopards on humans are rare, however injured, sick, or struggling individuals may turn to human flesh. The "Leopard of Panar" is reported to have killed as many as 400 people in northern India in the early years of the twentieth century.

Wolf
Like any large predator, a wolf is potentially dangerous, and common sense tells us to avoid them. Fortunately, attacks on people are very rare. Wolves with the disease rabies, in the "furious" stage, are the most dangerous.

DANGEROUS PLANTS

Plants have evolved a range of effective defences against animals that might want to eat them. Some need just the lightest touch and you're in trouble.

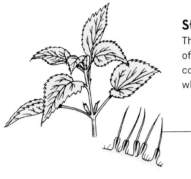

Stinging nettle

This plant is common in many temperate parts of the world. Hairs on the leaves and stems contain irritating chemicals, which are released when the plant comes into contact with skin.

stinging hairs

Cacti

Large cactus spines can be removed with tweezers. Work slowly because some spines have barbed ends. To remove very small, fine spines, apply duct tape to the area, then gently remove it.

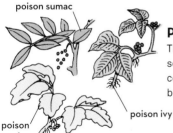

poison sumac

Poison ivy, poison oak, and poison sumac

These plants grow in parts of the United States and southern Canada. People react differently if they come into contact with them, but most will be affected by rashes and blistering.

poison ivy

poison oak

Stinging trees

There are about 37 species of stinging trees across Southeast Asia, Australia, and the Pacific Islands. Avoid the Australian Gympie-Gympie, as one touch can mean months of agonizing pain.

QUICKSAND

Quicksand is a mass of fine sand, silt, and clay that has become completely saturated with water. While it's hard to get out of, it is possible to escape.

1 If you feel yourself sinking into quicksand, act fast.

2 Unstrap your pack or any other heavy gear and throw it aside.

3 Drop onto your back to spread your weight. Then, work to free your legs.

4 Use swimming or snake-like motions to return to solid ground. It may take hours to move a few feet, but you can take a break at any time.

BEAR SAYS

Escaping from quicksand is a battle. The number one rule is to keep calm. Once you have escaped, clean yourself off to prevent further harm from chafing.

SOURCING WATER

If you are lost or your supplies are running low, your first task should be to find water. In some places water is easily found, but in arid (very dry) areas it can be a life-or-death challenge.

Animal indicators

birds flying low and fast

many animal tracks leading downhill

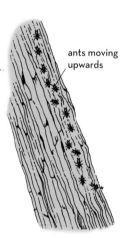
ants moving upwards

Follow the animals

All living things need water to survive. Observe the animals in your surroundings and you will get valuable clues. Don't forget to look for plants. Unusually green plants in an arid landscape may indicate water just below the surface.

Ants in a row

A column of ants heading up a tree trunk may be heading to a reservoir of water.

Distance to water

Bees
Usually within 5 km (3 mi).

Flies
Usually within 2.5 km (1.5 mi).

Mosquitoes
Usually within 450 m (1,500 ft).

Frogs
Usually in the immediate area.

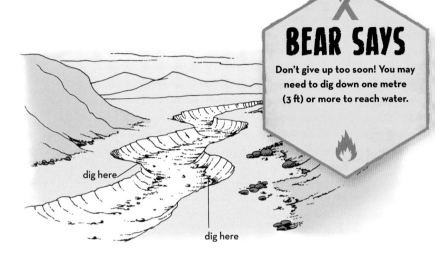

BEAR SAYS

Don't give up too soon! You may need to dig down one metre (3 ft) or more to reach water.

dig here

dig here

Dry riverbed

In a waterless landscape, a dry, sandy riverbed is often the best place to look for water. The best places to dig are the lowest points, the outside of bends, and near where green plants are growing.

dig here

dig here

Cliff base

Water naturally pools at the base of cliffs and hills. Such pools are deep and often the last to disappear because they are protected or partially protected from the sun. If no water is found, dig in places where it would pool after rain.

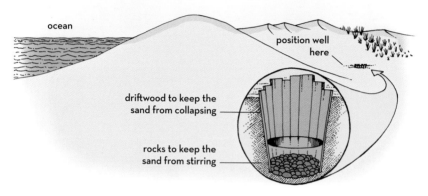

**driftwood to keep the
sand from collapsing**

**rocks to keep the
sand from stirring**

ocean

position well
here

Beach

A beach well is just a hole, dug behind the very first sand dune in from the ocean. It should be about one metre (3 ft) deep. Fresh groundwater seeping towards the ocean will gather in the well and float on top of the salty seawater.

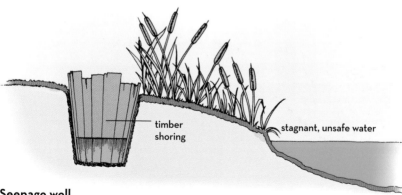

**timber
shoring**

stagnant, unsafe water

Seepage well

You may come across a stagnant body of water that is cloudy, has a bad flavour or odour, or is difficult to access. If this happens, dig a well about 10 m (30 ft) from the water source. The water that fills the well will be filtered and should be safe to drink.

WATER FROM PLANTS

If you can't find a water source in the environment around you, you can search for certain plants that can provide a drink.

machete

Green coconut
Slice open a green coconut with a sharp knife to access the water inside. Drink the coconut water in moderation because it is a natural laxative.

Mature coconut
Use a sharpened stake driven into the ground to split and remove the outer husk and reveal the shell. Drive a hole through a soft "eye" of the shell to access the coconut water.

stake

coconut husks

cut here

Banana tree
Cut through the trunk of a banana tree about 10 cm (4 in) above the ground. Then, hollow out a bowl-like reservoir inside the stump. Water from the roots will gather in the bowl. Scoop the water out of the bowl three times before drinking as the water will be bitter at first.

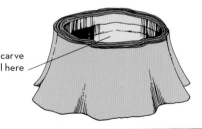

carve bowl here

Green bamboo

Green bamboo can supply you with fresh water, even at the height of the tropical dry season. To collect water from a young stalk, bend it over, tie it securely, and cut off the top. Water will drip out of the cut. Collect it in a container.

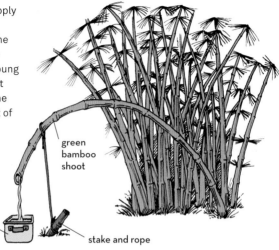

green bamboo shoot

collection container

stake and rope

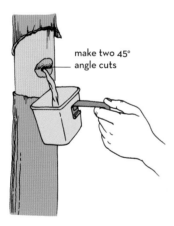

make two 45° angle cuts

Water from a vine

Cut a section of a vine high up. Then, sever it completely near the ground. Liquid will drain out the bottom. Don't drink from vines that produce white sap or milky liquid when cut. Get rid of liquid that has a sour or bitter taste.

Big bamboo

For larger shoots of green bamboo, simply cut a hole near the base of each section and collect the water within.

Transpiration

This is one of the most efficient and easily constructed sources of water in an arid setting. Tie a plastic bag around a leafy branch of a medium-sized tree or shrub, and place a container underneath. After a few hours in the sun, you will have some clean, drinkable water.

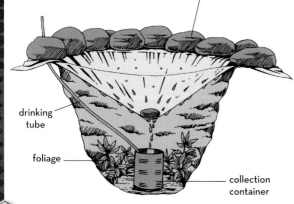

BEAR SAYS

Finding clean, safe water should always be your top priority. You can survive three weeks without eating, but only three days without water, so find it fast.

earth or rocks to weigh down the plastic sheet

drinking tube

foliage

collection container

Solar still

This system extracts water from the soil and any plants growing in or placed in a hole. Moisture evaporates, rises, and then condenses on the underside of the plastic barrier above, which then drips into a collection container below.

Water from cuttings

Collect as many green leaves and branches as can fit in a plastic bag without touching the sides. Prop up the centre to form a tent. Arrange the bag on a slight slope so the condensation will run down to a collection point.

padded stick

green cuttings

rocks to keep the vegetation elevated

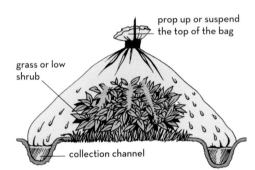

prop up or suspend the top of the bag

grass or low shrub

collection channel

Ground transpiration

This arrangement works on the same principle as the transpiration bag opposite, but with plants that grow close to the ground. Consider scaling up from a plastic bag by using the fly of a tent.

Cacti

Cacti are a valuable survival resource in many deserts. The fruits of the prickly pear and some other species are edible. Many cacti contain huge amounts of water in their flesh that can be gathered in solar stills or transpiration bags. Cacti are protected in some areas and should only be used in an emergency.

saguaro

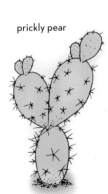

prickly pear

WATER PURIFICATION

In the wild, even water that looks pure and pristine may not be. Luckily, having clean drinking water is relatively simple when you have the right equipment and knowledge.

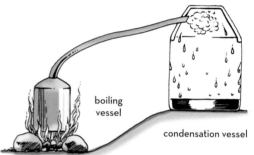

boiling vessel

condensation vessel

Distil

This system is trickier than simple boiling, but it makes drinkable water from sources heavy with sediment. It can also be used to distill seawater or urine.

Boil

This kills most types of disease-causing organisms. Boil the water for at least one minute, then let it cool down.

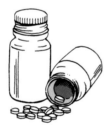

Chemical

Iodine, potassium permanganate, and chlorine can be used to treat water. They take time to work, and be prepared for a slightly odd taste.

Solar

Pour suspect water into clear plastic bottles and expose them to direct sunlight for at least six hours (or for two days in very cloudy conditions).

Filters

Thorough water filtration removes particles and many microorganisms that cause disease, but it's still a good idea to boil the water before drinking it.

water

gravel

sand

charcoal

BEAR SAYS

If you don't have a filter, you can make one using a plastic bottle, gravel, sand, and charcoal. The charcoal helps to filter out tiny impurities in the water.

virus and bacteria filter

parasite filter

carbon filter

Bottle filter

This filter bottle works with a cartridge that needs to be replaced after every 160 refills, or 216 gallons of water. Simply squeeze to produce a flow of water.

UV light emitter

Pump filter

There are many pump filtration systems that hikers can use. Each stroke of the pump draws water through the filter and purifies it.

pump handle

activated carbon

Ultraviolet

This battery-driven device uses UV light to sterilize 975 ml (33 oz) of water in 90 seconds. The water must be clear for the sterilization to work well.

FOOD FROM PLANTS

So you're stuck in the wilderness, and you've got plenty of safe drinking water. Your next priorities will probably be food and shelter. Plants can provide great nutrition if you know what's safe to eat.

Edibility test

1 Crush and smell the plant sample. Reject it if you sense strong, acid, or almond odours.

2 Crush and rub the sample against the inside of your elbow. Wait 15 minutes and discard if there is any irritation.

3 Hold a small amount against your lips. Reject if there is any irritation.

4 Place a small amount on the tongue. If there is any bad taste or irritation, throw it away.

5 Chew a small amount for several minutes, but do not swallow. If there is any irritation, spit it out.

6 If the plant part passes all these tests, eat a small amount and wait several hours for any adverse reaction.

BEAR SAYS

Tap along a piece of bamboo and listen to the noise it makes. Sections that have water inside will make a denser sound.

Split

Separate the plant into its basic components and test separately.

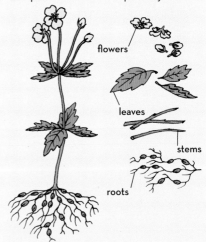

flowers

leaves

stems

roots

Plants to avoid

Some plants should be avoided altogether. Look for these indicators and leave them alone.

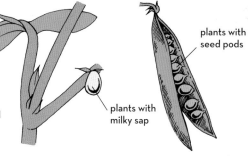

plants with seed pods

plants with milky sap

umbrella-shaped flower clusters

mushroom and toadstools – unless you are absolutely sure it is a safe species

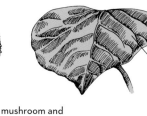
plants with shiny leaves

Plants to eat?

Most foods eaten by primates and birds are safe for us to eat, too. But this is not a guarantee – always use the edibility test opposite. Many berries are safe to eat, but only take a bite if you are certain they are edible, such as blackberries.

HUNTING SMALL ANIMALS

In a survival situation, a meal of meat goes a lot further than plants alone. While large animals can be difficult and dangerous to hunt, their smaller relatives are easier to get onto your plate.

Hand weapons
These are some tools traditionally used to catch small animals.

throwing stick

weighted club

rock

slingshot

bola

rodent skewer

BEAR SAYS

Insects, frogs, lizards, and snakes are a good source of protein. Keep tiredness at bay with these energy sources in an emergency.

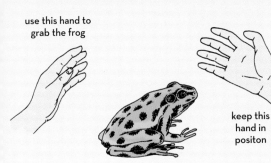

use this hand to grab the frog

keep this hand in positon

Catch a frog

Hold one hand about 50 cm (1.5 ft) in front of the frog and slowly wriggle your fingers. This will grab the frog's attention. Grasp the frog from behind with your other hand.

Catch a lizard

Gently wave a noose of tight wire in front of the lizard. Gradually bring the noose closer and closer, then lasso the lizard.

stout stick

forked stick

Catch a snake

All snakes can be eaten. To catch a snake, first stun it with a rock or stick. Pin its head down with a forked stick, and kill it with a knife, rock, or another stick. Cut the head off and bury it if there is any chance that it might be a venomous species.

Snares

These traps are used to catch some animals, often using wire or cord.

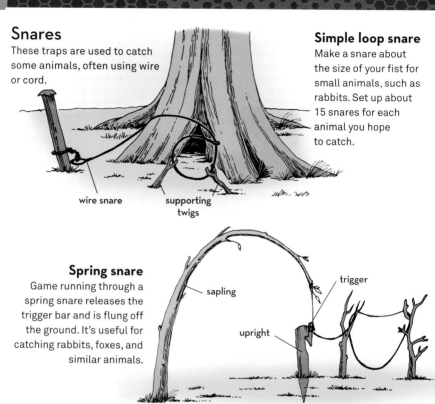

wire snare

supporting twigs

Simple loop snare

Make a snare about the size of your fist for small animals, such as rabbits. Set up about 15 snares for each animal you hope to catch.

Spring snare

Game running through a spring snare releases the trigger bar and is flung off the ground. It's useful for catching rabbits, foxes, and similar animals.

sapling

trigger

upright

close up of snare

Squirrel pole

A squirrel pole is a long pole placed against a tree. Place several wire nooses along the top and sides of the pole so that a squirrel trying to go up or down the pole will have to pass through one or more.

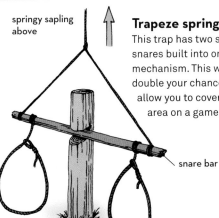

springy sapling above

Trapeze spring snare

This trap has two separate snares built into one mechanism. This will double your chances, or allow you to cover more area on a game trail.

snare bar

BEAR SAYS

In my experience it is always best to set as many traps as possible so that you have a greater chance of catching a meal.

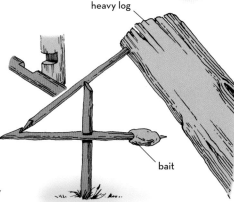

heavy log

Figure-4 deadfall trap

This simple trap can be made to any size. A horizontal bait bar is balanced at right angles to an upright with a lock bar, which supports a rock or other heavy weight.

bait

heavy log

retaining bar

trip line

Deadfall trap

It's easy to build a deadfall trap large enough to kill a pig or deer. Make sure everyone in the party knows exactly where such a trap has been set as it could also harm a person.

EDIBLE INVERTEBRATES

Insects, molluscs, and arachnids can be found in large quantities and they are highly nutritious. If survival is at stake, put your taste buds aside and add some of these critters to the menu.

Worms

There are few better sources of protein than worms. Drop them in drinkable water after collection and they will naturally wash themselves out. If you `prefer, dry and grind the worms and add them to soup.

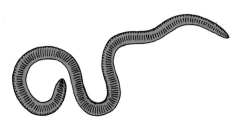

Snails

Starve snails for a few days so they can expel any poisonous plants they have eaten. Boil them for three minutes then drain, rinse in cold water, and remove from their shells. Avoid species with brightly coloured shells.

Spiders

Don't overlook spiders as a source of protein. Eat the bodies and leave the heads, which may contain poison. If you catch a tarantula, try frying it – they are a delicacy in parts of Southeast Asia.

Slugs

Some slugs are very large – three or four will constitute a good meal. They can be eaten raw, but are much more appetizing cooked. Prepare and cook them exactly the same way as snails.

Grubs

Insect larvae, also known as grubs, are prime wilderness food. They favour cool, damp places, so look in rotten logs, under the bark of dead trees, under rocks, and in the ground. Grubs are safe to eat raw.

Grasshoppers

These insects can be a great source of food in some places. Knock them from the air with a piece of clothing or a leafy branch. Remove the wings, antennae, and legs before eating them. It is best to roast them to kill off any parasites.

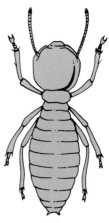

Termites

These insects exist in enormous numbers in the warmer parts of the world and are easily collected from their nests. Remove the wings from larger species before eating. They can be cooked, but are more nutritious eaten raw.

Aquatic insects

Nearly all water-based insects can be eaten in both adult and larval form. Use clothing as a net and trawl freshwater rivers or ponds.

EMERGENCY SHELTERS

Hot or cold, wet or dry, a good shelter is vital for your safety. Each landscape requires different types of shelter. Use the natural resources at hand depending on your need.

Desert shelter
Dig a hollow and cover with two tarpaulins one above the other.

entrance

insulation

All-natural shelter
A leafy bed, brush-covered lean-to, and a fire can keep you warm and dry.

Bough bed
A bough bed is made from evergreen branches arranged in overlapping rows. It will provide insulation, comfort, and will keep you above any rain that is running along the ground.

logs to keep the boughs in place

Fallen tree shelter

A fallen tree can make a quick shelter. Improve it by removing branches on the underside and slinging a tarpaulin on top.

check that the broken part is strong enough to last the night

tie the tops together

Sapling shelter

If you come across a group of saplings, clear the ground between them, strip their branches, and tie their tops together. Cover with material or weave branches between them.

hold up the "roof" with extra branches

weigh down the covering

BEAR SAYS

In harsh weather or desperate situations, shelters such as these can save your life!

Tree pit snow shelter

In forests where heavy snow has fallen, you will often find deep hollows under the branches of evergreen trees. Dig out some extra room if needed, and lay branches on the ground.

Discover more amazing books in the Bear Grylls series:

Perfect for young adventurers, the
Survival Skills series accompanies an
exciting range of colouring and activity
books. Curious kids can also learn
tips and tricks for almost any extreme
situation in *Survival Camp*, and explore
Earth in *Extreme Planet*.

Conceived by Weldon Owen in partnership
with Bear Grylls Ventures

Produced by Weldon Owen Ltd
Suite 3.08 The Plaza, 535 King's Road,
London SW10 0SZ, UK

Copyright © 2017 Weldon Owen Publishing

WELDON OWEN LTD
Publisher Donna Gregory
Designer Shahid Mahmood
Editorial Claire Philip, Sophia Podini
Illustrators Peter Bull Studios (original illustrations),
Bernard Chau (colour)

Printed in Malaysia

10 9 8 7 6 5 4 3 2 1

All rights reserved. No part of this publication may be reproduced, stored in a retrieval system
or transmitted in any form by any means, electronic, mechanical, photocopying, recording or
otherwise, except brief extracts for the purpose of review, without the prior
written permission of the publisher.

Disclaimer
Weldon Owen and Bear Grylls take pride in doing our best to get the facts right in putting together
the information in this book, but occasionally something slips past our beady eyes. Therefore we
make no warranties about the accuracy or completeness of the information in the book and to the
maximum extent permitted, we disclaim all liability. Wherever possible, we will endeavour to correct
any errors of fact at reprint.

Kids – if you want to try any of the activities in this book, please ask your parents first! Parents – all
outdoor activities carry some degree of risk and we recommend that anyone participating in these
activities be aware of the risks involved and seek professional instruction and guidance. None of the
health/medical information in this book is intended as a substitute for professional medical advice;
always seek the advice of a qualified practitioner.

A WELDON OWEN PRODUCTION.
PART OF THE BONNIER PUBLISHING GROUP.